PRAISE

Warble encompasses the poetry of connection to the life force, weaving and unraveling immersions into grief and birth, presence and yearning, mother love and father loss, blossom and flight. These poems are compelling, brave, intimate, and, most of all, unafraid of telling the truth. I found that once I started reading them, I couldn't stop, and I was called back to re-read many stunning dives into the tender and fierce edges of life, such as the complex compassion in "Addling," the daring energy in "Open Water," and the breathless love of "You Ask Me to Tell You the Story." The title itself—*Warble*—speaks to that in-between state (as well as a bird) of being alive, trilling through each poem.

I picked this collection because of how deeply the poet wrote from what Edward Hirsch calls "the poetry of affection," the poetry that connect us to our innate and vulnerable humanness. This quality is so vital when it comes to working with the fragments of brokenness, despair, and horror around us to craft a life, sustain a community, and behold the living earth with wonder and courage.

—Caryn Mirriam-Goldberg, 2024 Birdy Poetry Prize Judge, Poet Laureate of Kansas (2009-2013), author of *How Time Moves: New & Selected Poems*

Warble

Winner of The Birdy Poetry Prize—2024
by Meadowlark Press

WARBLE

Alicia Rebecca Myers

MEADOWLARK PRESS

Celebrating 10 Years
established 2014

EMPORIA, KANSAS

Meadowlark Press, LLC
meadowlarkbookstore.com
P.O. Box 333, Emporia, KS 66801

Warble

Cover design by Richard Kegler

Author photo by Macy Smolsky

Interior design by Linzi Garcia, Meadowlark Press

POETRY / American / General
POETRY / Subjects & Themes / Nature
POETRY / Subjects & Themes / Family

ISBN: 978-1-956578-65-2
Library of Congress Control Number: 2024952519

for my parents

I got through all of last year

and I'm here

—**Stephen Sondheim,** *Follies*

CONTENTS

I

Ringer | 3

Hot Horse | 4

The Last Travel Agent | 5

Open Water | 6

Giving Birth May Alter a Mother's Bones | 7

Homeschool | 8

Migration | 11

Legs | 12

The Real Housewives of the Anthropocene | 14

Pod | 15

Cans & | 16

Hot Peppers | 17

The Vine | 18

Head-On | 19

Mouth to Spring | 20

G Day | 21

The Surprise | 22

Closed Composition | 23

Alternate | 24

II

The Difference | 27

The Thirteenth Guest | 28

Commerce in Absence | 29

Piano Tuning | 30

They Are Alive and Well Somewhere | 31

The Tongue Also is a Fire | 32

America Runs On | 33

When You Hear It, You Will Know | 34

Dominoes | 35

My Child's Optimism | 36

Postscript | 37

No Choice | 38

Grieving | 39

Remembrance Plaque | 40

The Other Side | 41

What's the Costliest Thing You've Ever Dropped? | 42

Service | 43

Only | 44

Sex After Death | 45

Obol | 46

Castles | 47

In This Together | 48

Black Hole | 49

Beautiful from the Dead | 50

Revelations | 51

Guy | 52

National Museum of Mathematics | 53

III

January | 57

Periodic | 58

Easy | 59

Scotch Egg, Black Kazoo, Grandmother's Ghost | 60

Sea Glass | 61

Addling | 62

Perimenopause | 64

My Parents' Lives Before Mine | 65

There Are No Words | 66

Moth Spotted Sipping a Sleeping Bird's Tears | 67

Parked Car | 69

Latter-Day Comfort | 70

Rare Bird | 71

Uncountable | 72

Love Island | 73

Lexaprode | 74

Thank You | 75

Idiot Birdwalk | 77

Resurrection | 78

Anniversary | 79

Homestay | 80

Men | 81

You Ask Me to Tell You the Story | 82

Closing | 84

First Day | 85

Warble | 86

Loss | 87

Hawks on Light Posts | 88

Triptych | 90

Publication Acknowledgments | 93

Personal Acknowledgments | 94

About the Author | 95

I

Ringer

I would never want to be 25 again,
bandana for a shirt, parading like some fire-breathing
dragon prop that accidentally caught on fire.

Now, I am my own magician. Every morning, I pull
colorful dog poop bags out of my pocket.
The trick is I have lived. I buried a father, pushed

a 9.4 pound baby out of my vagina. His head
was so big I begged my midwife
to kill me. His crown appeared and withdrew

incrementally, until the hair stayed put long enough
for me to pet it. That shift was so deliciously
medieval, so wildly beautiful, I could never return

to self-doubt: switchback period of blowing
clove smoke out the window to John Mayer,
thinking, *What did I do wrong?* When I answered

an ad to sit in an unmarked van and guard handbells
for eight hours, I could have been making
my own music.

Hot Horse

The guidebook said to look for an orange box. We strolled through Tivoli Park, past the pond, past the mansion guarded by its four cast iron dogs. Story goes that their sculptor shot himself for forgetting their tongues. I, for one, will never forget my tongue. I take it everywhere I go. I wanted a fast horse, wanted to play karst to some fierce-muscled Lipizzan, to ingest, via burger, gait's tracery. We queued up inside the kiosk. You recused yourself from gloppy nacho condiment. I handled a bun big as a moon, the meat thin and tough and smeared with ajvar. My ring against the former runner glimmered. How to say this? Like a castle of gristle. Like lake effect in the gut. My love for you the inverse of the trapped feeling. I later read about the man who climbed atop the roof of his dead father's car as thieves sped it away, and thought: *Yes*. He held on ferociously. A herd of grief moving through him. This is how I cling to memory. The trees: just blurs. We met Tomaž by Dragon Bridge for dinner. In the only photo I have of us, he's wearing a checkered Polo shirt. *To your honeymoon*, he said, then sang the praises of the marinated horse steak. I ordered one. This was only hours after Hot Horse, two years before he died. There are boxes and there are boxes. I keep welcoming wildness inside me.

The Last Travel Agent

She hides honey in a globe.
Her hair smells of camphor.
Mornings, children scatter
heirlooms. Their fingers work the ash.
Here is a mesh of lace. Here is a rope
of felt. Sometimes, the stones become the fragile
cups and saucers she once laid out for friends.
Remember the sky
strewn with paper lanterns?
The moon as anything other
than dread? O bird with one wing
heavier than the other.

Air splinters. Like a Medusa head
the capstan glowers.
Geography is spent.
Line them up, line them up.
How does the fable go again? Enough stones
in the pitcher and the crow can drink.

Open Water

If blubber could absorb it, if con men could fleece it,
if stand-ins could raze it, if only the government
hadn't made a black lung out of every exit,
every option. More hologram
insignia: a passel of bald eagles hovers right
beneath the contrails, their tails at full
salute like a proxy indicator
of irradiance. You contemplate the difference
between *threshold* and *crossed*. Algae blooms
blossom against your wrists. A man shouts,
You shouldn't be in there! You used to acclimate
to lake temperature by drawing
a cold bath. Now, pulling through this tepid
soup in winter's wake, air expelled
in gasps, you listen out for the drone
of bullfrogs breathing through their skin,
immersed chorus of debris, their bodies
incrementally rising to the surface. The marker
of a pocked silo helps you sight
the shoreline. You stay
on course, circumscribed and awash
in melon light. You'd rather put on your favorite
A-line dress (the one with Monet's Garden at Giverny print)
and twirl in a rush of iris, forget
each moment when carbon dioxide meets infrared,
but you don't. You swim.

Giving Birth May Alter a Mother's Bones

It isn't the depletion of calcium and phosphorus that leaves me
unable to stand at times but the world. My liver is a river bed,
my uterus a planetary nebula. My lungs have become
secondary to your survival. When I try to sleep, I feel my marrow
weeping. What swaths of toxic stew will you inherit? There is nothing
I wouldn't offer up on my platelets if it meant you might
not suffer. Right now, sick on the couch
watching walkthroughs, you can't possibly know the extent
of my changed pancreas or that my brain was refashioned into
a crouching lioness when you were born. I only recognize
my heart because you carry it.

Homeschool

1

You pronounce that when the body goes,
the head doesn't.
A dog comes back as a cat,
a cat as another cat
with the same name. That faraway
look is you working through some first
falling-off: narrowed breath, fixed blood.
In the bath you empty one container
into another, ask me to explain
how the soul rises.

2

Some animals play dead. Some children move
equally between monster and doctor.
A possum will emit convincing mucus
like a rotting carcass. You go limp
behind the sprinkler, admit
it's all pretend when I sprint over
clutching a cut iris. Young fire ants
feign death intuiting
the limits of their soft
exoskeleton. *Give me that flower!*
you yell, and I toss it onto your chest
like an aficionada.

3

Divide and subtract your world,
learn to reduce by things. I take away
two crayons, leaving you
with three. I make an abacus out of Adoration
Tomatoes (agreed: that our mouths will be
zero). Why 500 miles on a plane
feels different than in a car is a question I answer
by invoking wings. I worry your grandparents
won't live much longer. They keep trying
to give me furniture.
If I pinch the skin
on the back of my hand it takes seconds
to retract. We spend days testing
each other's age this way—the sharp pain,
the sudden tent.

4

Sidewalk chalk suffuses the dead
centipede with flux and incandescence—pink residue
dusting the basin
that holds the end
of something. I think, how
can I be frank about each limb
in your outstretched palm?

5

Moonlight enters through your blinds, casting
transverse stripes. I pray that somewhere
hidden and hushed a thylacine hunts.
That the curved horns of an aurochs brighten
against its curls. Most nights, I can't believe my luck
you exist. I would like to confess
I sneak into your room
to kiss your widow's peak,
but you already know this. Encircling my neck
with sleepy arms you've caught me. A world
in which you learn the word *snare*
but still insist on *aminal*:
Why can't I have both?

6

That you never die is the eyelash wish
whispered in my ear. And when the hair
disappears from your finger, I lie:
that our demise is like the catatonic
trick of sharks. That our breath slows,
not stops—the spirit soldered
so expertly to our lungs—

Migration

Viewed at night and from high above, 64,000 green sea turtles resemble floating stars, making the Great Barrier Reef like a second firmament to the human eye. Some of their carapaces are painted with a bright white stripe. They can't spot this on themselves or communicate their knowledge of another's markings. Turtles are short-sighted. They look up and mistake the sky for ocean. Their distant counterparts waver back as bony light. What keeps them going, alone and in aggregate, is believing every star to be a shell.

Legs

The ocean was popular and nearby removed
        from her like an ablation her grandmother
warned that she would be removed from *it* her body
                                    excised from water
what happened was different

an emptying out   as if she'd contained all
along that which she'd lived in like a rainbow
in a portrait of a saint
        whose heart has been rent and   lifted

the patina of silent repetition
  deafening   first she touched toes to lips
an algae bloom of blood what was it about
legs that she'd wanted so badly   something to do
          with the soul   she could feel his soul against her chest
                            as he almost drowned
the thin cloud of it her almost soul on the temple floor
     straightening his legs like oars to scull her into eternity   genitalia
were nothing new tender pressure-center
in her tail   spot that shimmered in the phosphorescence of yellow fin
                  fusiliers   a school of them   darting
           in and out of hushed coral
                  that only revealed its color when in proximity

        to light she was light
with legs   what did it mean to live
        forever legs legs legs her knees were a rosary

she kissed morning noon and night but especially night
when God appeared a gelatinous eye
blinking a metronome demanding that she dance

  awake she felt the water pouring out
                asleep the same
between her legs the memory of basin   nautilus
                                 sharks as mammoth as sunken
          vessels   hydrothermal vents like chimneys
   migration sounds

once the surface of the ocean turned
     milky miles and miles of pale tundra she'd wished that she could walk on
  more than walk   kneel
                she'd wished that she could kneel before

such pure absolution examining the hole between her legs she wondered if this is where
the soul will enter
    when it does she wound
her braid she thought a prayer
Dear Lord   Dear Liege Dear Legs

The Real Housewives of the Anthropocene

Kim says the demise of plants hurts her feelings. After Harper's lunar mining business goes under, Isla bitches in her confessional, "She can't even keep a thin atmosphere." Evelyn's husband's cheating scandal briefly unites the women. Kim gives her a digital copy of the genome of an extinct crested gecko, and together, they drink reserve gin in Evelyn's luxury bunker. The two make fun of Camilla for thinking desertification is a pop-up cakery. Harper gets addicted to Fusion Power diet pills, slurs on camera, "I wish paper were still a thing!!" Camilla's teenage daughter hosts a seance; the wrong spirits come. Roz returns from overseas philanthropy with her maize charity, only to discover several ladies have raised money for sugarcane instead. Isla gets drunk, points a finger at Roz, screams, "Automated slut!" Harper debuts her new Smart Shoe line with her new Smart Face. When the storm comes, they hire help to board up the windows of their gated community with blingy plywood. They listen to the wind. They ask not to film this part.

Pod

It's as if placing a boundary in between people has actually removed a boundary.
—Paul, *Love Is Blind* Season 4

Love is patient, love is kind
of like when an aquarium octopus escapes to find another
octopus obstructing the drain pipe. My grandfather who glued
his eye to the circus tent's striped canvas to view a woman
removing her stockings was more smitten with the lines
of limitation. Any relatively narrow causeway
and my imagination swells like the waves
the concrete keeps me from. The clasp
of my bra has been both polished door knocker and impediment
to horn-mad fingers. I have watched an invisible wall become
more believable when the mime took advantage of a fixed point, keeping
one hand motionless, unlike the full body swaying that happens in
slow dancing. This was years ago, on the streets
of Paris. If God were to rend my veil, well,
I would probably hate it.

Cans &

This morning, I watched a robin convert a pothole into a bird bath,
the kind of fearless ingenuity I covet. I ask myself why Rothko listened to
his doctor when advised not to paint color blocks higher than a yard
because of his heart ailment. Did acrylic on paper suddenly convey more
intimate spiritual planes? I don't know enough about art or spiritual planes
to say, although one time, at the Dalí museum in Figueres, I stood on my head
in front of the wall-size rendering of Gala and sprung the roots branching
down from her bare chest skyward. There is a lockstep to daily life
that can be subverted: the huzzah! of reconfiguring the pattern, of houndstooth
disrupted by gingham to create an intermediate state. On 34B, the sign for the bar
that is also a trailer reads *Cans & Clams* or *Cans &* or *& Clams*, depending on
availability, and I love that, the not knowing, the big marquee, the shifting
language, the discovery made possible every drive.

Hot Peppers

Without announcing it, I leave the dinner table
to go in search of hot peppers. A hollowed-out
black walnut like a helmet nearly trips me,
but I remove my shoes, plunge a big toe
into its crevice. I think about my parents
selling their house. I bet they were elated
when they first brought me home
from the hospital. Now what. At night,
I go through my son's backpack and stuff
his artwork in the trash, hide it
at the bottom, because minimalists teach us
process matters more than paper. I've bitten
into three peppers already and can't find one
hot enough. I call out to our feral cat
over the hum of an emerging brood
of cicadas. Riverbank grape vines
overrun our brick oven. Earlier on the phone,
my mom said, *Do you want*
the guest bed? What about those flowers
preserved behind glass? I can't visualize,
so I asked her to describe them in more
detail. *You know. Pressed.*
I want to make this easier for them.
I agree to take what I can.

The Vine

You tell me I should write about a vine. *I'll try*, I say. My therapist, a former stand-up comic, has also given me an assignment: Jot down scenes that spring to mind when you think about your childhood. I'm unsure which one to do first, so I do neither. I boil the water for strong coffee. I remember when you were five and asked me what matters more to me: making people laugh or making sure the house doesn't burn down. Later, I justify my margin and start the poem. In third grade, I climbed on top of the monkey bars and panicked. Recess was suddenly over; my classmates left me there. I shook from feeling trapped while also respecting the existential hilarity in the horizontal bars being an unusable ladder. God is funny haha. This twinning might be how I see the world in general. I could cry myself to sleep knowing my parents are moving into Senior Living, but when I think of the misplaced handgun in their attic, laugh instead. It's like terrestrial radio, this sensation of being broadcast while also tied to the ground. My therapist adjusted her exercise to be less visual because my aphantasia is a kind of mental blindness. I resisted the urge to tell her a painful joke, the one about braille and a cheese grater. Sometimes I sprawl across the bed in sadness. Sometimes I choke with laughter.

Head-On

What does the middle of the ocean sound like
as you're rowing away from it
I get up in the deep of night
for a drink of water
tired of facing
every empirical crisis
when I think of nothingness
it isn't the whopping ocean
but silent nitrate films
burning in a warehouse
walking along the shore
with a loaf of bread tucked under my arm
for my dad to use a hook-bait
I watched his line for a bit
but soon grew bored
so much I never thought to ask him
did you feel anything even if
you didn't catch anything

Mouth to Spring

Our foster puppy lacks restraint. He leads with his gibbous
stomach. He gums first shoots and nibbles ephemerals.
A favorite snack is Glory-of-the-Snow, so named
because it flowers early. For a canapé, he unearthed last year's
Easter egg, still hidden. When he's especially naughty, I taunt him
with stories of Six Mile Creek and Sapsucker Woods where
fragile bloodroot grows. He's never been. Sometimes, I talk to him
about things that aren't so pretty. Tell him how the branching
nodules seen in a thoracic scan are called tree-in-bud opacity.

G Day

Today is G Day, my son says to me
the morning after another school shooting
he doesn't yet know about. The alphabet countdown
has begun to mark the passage of time between
now and the final class when second graders stream
out the guarded door and into summer. *We're learning
about grapes*, he says, and as I unknot his hair,
hands shaking, I picture the kids in a criss-cross
circle, eyes closed, each biting excitedly into
a succulent spherical berry before giving language
to the pop: *sweet and tart* or *like jelly*. And there
will certainly be a child who thinks but maybe doesn't
say, *the shape of a bullet*, the way his teacher will keep
her terror private, the way I hear in my head, *G is for gun*.

The Surprise

My father died two weeks before
his 48ᵗʰ wedding anniversary. What ate up
my mother was the fact that he had
planned a special dinner for it
but never told her details, just a sweet
allusion: *It's a surprise.* I must have
called every restaurant in the days
following for proof of reservation,
strange to ask, *Do you have record
of a past name*, wondering where
they would have sat, his order, if
acute leukemia would have stopped
him from drinking beer or
pointing to the slabs of beef
wheeled out on a silver cart and
saying, *That one.* But no one
could find him: not the Peddler
Steakhouse, not the Angus Barn, not
Mandolin. Not even Red Lobster.
What a bureaucratic waste my grief
made of time. I held my breath
whenever a person answered.

Closed Composition

Before photography or video, people
were rendered in portraiture: how they
stood, how they sat. A yawn was rarely
captured. If you misremembered after
they were gone, that was that.

Alternate

Where antlers shake free the moose. Where
corals reproduce
quickly. Luminous mosses glow inward and
invisibly, waves
dictate the moon's undulation. Touch the
beating elephant heart
without wearing gloves. Inside each nesting
doll, a larger doll.
Cordoning is obsolete, as is bulk upheaval.
Deep-sea brine pools into polar sanctuaries.
Cursed are those who mourn.
The dead are still alive.

II

The Difference

Why did you throw out all my baby albums, I asked my mom
who said, *I thought you didn't want them*, said,
I took them to the landmine. She gripped my hands
across your body like one-half the burden of a whipsaw,
cried she wasn't sure, what if you could still walk, refused
to administer the morphine or leave the room, changed
the pillow cases, Vaselined your lips. I leaned into
one of your two bad ears to tell you I read birds
are immune to chili pepper heat, gave you permission to go,
at night laid down on your side of the bed to follow
your irregular breathing through the cracked door
while binge-watching *Love Island* episodes on mute.
Mom, come look at the supermoon, the same
as when I gave birth in a baby storm, but she wouldn't.

The Thirteenth Guest

I'm talking with you more now than when you were here.
12 months in a year, a single day made up of two 12-hour blocks,
time compartmentalized into even stops and starts like benignant
edits to a hackneyed personal statement. My student emails back,
My counselor thinks it shows too much privilege to admit I hike
the Alps every summer, I'm thinking, *Go ahead then, change it*
to a single Alp, the world obsessed with revision, luck, the way I care
more about what one relative crossed out in her sympathy card
than the actual visible sentiment. God, I hated how you voted, vice
versa, you never understood how I saw the shape of mid-morning light
through the window, quiet conspirator, your ideology like the heirloom
staff of a butter churn, every Thanksgiving that you carved the bird
was as if I rolled in late for supper, unleavened gospel, left-wing attitude.

Commerce in Absence

Sheets need to be purchased for hospice. Inside fluorescent
Bed, Bath, and Beyond, I debate between Egyptian cotton
and cheaper weave, timeline kept at bay at check-out, one day,
two days most. Coffee, cajun chicken filet biscuit combo (no taste
for either), bulk Bounty paper towels and Diet Coke from BJ's,
impulse bluetooth headphones that work by transmitting signals
over short distances. Obsessed with your crossing over, I put
When Breath Becomes Air into my cart but don't order, apprentice
at the funeral home lingers on a Powerpoint slide with low-cost options
for tossing your ashes, ever-orbit or eternal reef. The highs of retail
therapy lead me into Anthropologie for a $200 black maxi dress
marketed as sensual, subtle.

Piano Tuning

Front covers removed, hammers and action exposed,
my technician tells me he's tuning the strings of a single note
to themselves. He opens up about his family while sounding
intervals: former fiancée, new fiancée, neighbor's seven kids
intent on scaling walls. What matters is you stabilize
the pitch. I wrote down everything you said those nights I waited
by your electric bed, mind stripped clean, allegro of
delirium: *How do I plant memory? What mode am I in?*
You pointed to a flock of sheep running toward a huge waterfall,
little girl on her mother's lap. Every word to me a crumb,
a key. *Now I'm timing beating partials.*

They Are Alive and Well Somewhere

And to die is different from what any one supposed, and luckier,
Whitman first wrote in 1855, then again in 1856, then another six times until
his deathbed revision. Once, I watched popcorn kernels continue to explode after
I took them off the fire, same day I read a rise in uncontrolled white blood cells causes leukemia.
Remember limbo, Kristy's third grade ice skating party, how you picked me up
early to tell me granddaddy passed? Me, thinking, my feet are cold but not permanently.
I never saw him buried. Nobody talked about it. A cousin suggested we play the board game
Ghosts, glow-in-the-dark pieces. State-mandated autopsy meant I sat with your corpse
hours after you died, occasionally held your hand, cried, ate chocolate-covered fruit
over your dead body, you clearly gone, the gift of seeing that difference, final edit.

The Tongue Also is a Fire

Centralia burns. Miles of labyrinthine mines of smoke and lethal
flames that buckled roads and made a sinkhole town a visitor
might straddle, one foot hot, one foot temperate. I go to leave
my mark there. Forget scripture: high pressure can of aerosol
paint closer to bona fide elegy, hunched over that narrow strip
of Route 61 covered in graffiti, defiantly facing a horizon
of coal seam plumes, back to the living breathing other body
of phenomena, half in, half out, partial ground on fire, night
exhumed, all encompassing, then I might really write something.

America Runs On

A man at Dunkin' Donuts like my dad
in profile lifts a coffee to his lips,
commercials call it Dunkin' now, the *dun*,
the *kin*, I'm broken in that ceaseless way
a call no longer reaches him, not long
ago I phoned the hotline printed on
a box with my suggestion, *April is
the cruller month*, nobody responded.

When You Hear It, You Will Know

I lied before when I wrote *in profile*, I'm too compelled by song, couldn't sound
out the exactness of your gentle posture head-on, extant mustache, archtop eyes,
every poem an imperfect room, obsolete lighthouse, a record
you loved was *Bill Monroe Live at the Opry*, cued it up on Spotify,
that's not true, it was *Bluegrass Legends*, more impactful to include
live, better to recall every poem as an imperfect *measure*, another sound I will never
approximate is the death rattle, one Reddit user advised, *When you hear it, you will know.*

Dominoes

You tripped and broke your hip/waited on your side
for the ambulance/gone six days later/after we turned
your urn/to fit inside the niche/my mom found
next/askew in bed/unresponsive/ventilator and aortic
tear/the call came at Café Dewitt/farmhouse break-
fast/widowhood effect/I leaned against a wall/I slid down it

My Child's Optimism

At first seemed profligate, like every light left on
overnight in a lighting store, he streamered the living
room doorway in bright crepe paper, unnecessary
obstacle, I crawled under on my belly, *For the last time
stop doing this*, he laughed and said, *But you got through it.*

Postscript

After her husband took his final breath, my mother
notified the funeral home, 47 years of marriage, carefully
removed his hearing aids, opened up their closet, got dressed
in her finest linen jacket, smoothed out the wrinkles for company.

No Choice

You hadn't eaten, could barely swallow, I held
the bowl of ice cream eye-level, Neapolitan, just the three
of us, asked, *Which flavor?* Your mumble: *all of them.*

Grieving

One, two, buckle my shoe
Three, four, buckle my shoe

Remembrance Plaque

Guy Arnold Myers, Jr. (1936-2022)

The Other Side

She coded in the ICU, nurses brought her back, successful extubation, changed her paperwork to DNR, corrected the visiting pastor, *I don't have a daughter, only a sister.*

What's the Costliest Thing You've Ever Dropped?

I Google variations on the same pressing question. A contrite
writer begs, *Does it count if I backed into an ice sculpture?*
My therapist insists, *You can't carry her grief for her.*

Service

Mouthed "Shall We Gather At the River" from my pew, listened to "Long Ride Home" in the car, ordered fried pickles at the bar, drank bourbons from a smoking tumbler, practiced saying *died*, sang "Somewhere" with our waiter (musical theater major), got sloppy-metaphysical, kissed my partner, impersonated Pete's dragon, left to check on my mother, wished I wasn't her consoler.

Only

Only a combination of numbers and letters, only recollection, only in-person, only multiply, only uncontrollably, only guesses, only fits, only one true God, only partial eclipse, only months, only stays, only faxed, only shift, only remaining couple, only barely, only just, only delivery within a ten-mile radius, only flight available, only child, only document

Sex After Death

Grateful for a body but unsure what to do with it,
I draw my husband closer, I'm all angular momentum, figure
skater upright spinning, pleasure distant, policy wonk
on the television, like a cactus rustler, tentatively touch his skin, thieve
anodyne, worried your ghost is listening in, terrified the after-
life works this way, half-praying you might short the light, scandalized.

Obol

At the inventory of your safe deposit box, I counted out
the coins you'd secreted, three-cent pieces, Liberty Nickels, no fare
for Charon, numismatist, silver and copper and Confederate
bills alongside pages of your high school arithmetic, you were
the gaunt old man leaving me boat money, backward sacrament,
carved walking stick in your right hand, ambling under under-
story, oh how I wish you'd talked more, round mouth empty.

Castles

How do I mourn a parent I loved but wasn't close to, I mean how do I learn to let go
of what I longed for contrary to fact, I guess what I'm asking is, if falling back
is gaining an hour, how much time might be amassed by merely stopping, there are entire days
I don't care to sing, isn't it strange how blood transcends anger, as a travel agent
I once flew to Turkey, didn't bother to tell you, climbed terraces barefoot at Pamukkale,
the travertine hard but powdery in places like sugar-dusted pavlova, calcium carbonate
snow, my guidebook called them cotton castles, I was twenty-eight, I remember the far-
flung thrill of illuminated pools, my sovereignty in being a trace element, what did I know of distance.

In This Together

My mother is a storyteller, irritating clothing tag with gentle care
instructions, as a child nearly sat on a water moccasin, wasn't allowed
to see Elvis, unreliable narrator, at the widows support circle
chided another resident, *I didn't know we could talk about pet loss*, her outgoing
message a series of fumblings, sometimes I ignore her calls to speak with you instead, you never
relive your death with me sequentially, she likes to complain, *My daughter is a storyteller*, years ago
took me to the traveling Titanic exhibit, a docent handed us each a card with the name of a passenger,
we placed our hands on a block of ice meant to simulate tragedy, checked for our survival
against the final wall, surprise, we both made it.

Black Hole

Could you likewise translate into sound, light captured first as spit-up
data, then imperceptible frequency, then amplified and raised from
low-pitch? I bet there was a runner on every base when a slung bat
to the head left you permanently partially deaf. The most I've ever felt
like you was as a new mother. I got sick and lost some decibels. Bird calls
disappeared, not all, but forever. I drive your car now. My favorite Real
Housewife wrote in her memoir, *The dead slip out quietly
and leave furious holes in their wake.* It would be easier if they were audible,
the holes and the dead. When I open up the change holder to feed the meter,
I find a film canister full of the cotton balls you used to shield your ears from rain.

Beautiful from the Dead

The world gives us many gifts and some of them are tinged. There is a kind
of brazenness to dolor, Johnny Cash's untrained voice, *Well, I don't care if I do-*
die-do-die-do-die-do, cluster of baby spiders emerging from the plastic
pan flute my baby put his mouth to in the tub. Platen presses against paper
to leave an impression, isn't that a miracle? The same mother at her most vulnerable
stripping the sheets, gloves off, awash with misery, calls to tell me she wore
a mask to a masquerade ball. I could dually burst from pain and happiness. The hospital
emails an anesthesia survey, *How did we do?* I write back, *Too well*. This year
at Thanksgiving I burnt the oyster dressing, family recipe, but bit into a pearl. To not lose it,
stored it with my antidepressant. My son comes home and says, *June and I started a club,*
it's called Beautiful from the Dead, we take dead flowers and leaves and make them pretty again.

Revelations

My mother started writing poetry at age 81: *Sun shining on the glistening water,*
ducks swim by in a straight line. I quote her
back to her as a way to induce faith in unlooked-for
pick-me-ups. We startle every time at the motion
sensor animatronic parrot, it squawks when we walk by. I hold her hand
in front of the ATM, tell her, *You can do this*, she blinks before
her sudden independence like rays reflected off a lake of fire, my childhood
lake behind the home she lived in for over four decades. The last time we stood
together in that driveway, she crushed a baby snake with her heel. I was trying
to gather it with proof of insurance. I hesitate, ask her what she thinks
you were hoping to impart when you uttered, *Put five sea creatures in a box and see*
which one reacts to God's son, I just assumed Jesus. I'm haunted by the homophone.

Guy

You had a name that could have meant anyone, yet you were here and particular: layered
Vidalia onions you peeled and ate like apples, faint freckles on your belly, needles of Vidaza inserted
between them, after we saw *March of the Penguins* you signed your emails Father Penguin, attached
pics of squirrels and ticks and roof refurbishment, guns hidden in the ceiling, password to your tablet
my birthday, why did you over-photo document, chair56.jpg, some nights I fix a drink
and unsubscribe you from far-right propaganda, struggle with how to reconcile the whole with its parts,
in Indian Princesses we were Bald Eagle and White Dove, how do I separate love from what is
reprehensible, in 1975 you hunted a bear while camping along the White Water River, hunkered down
in the undercut of a logging road to avoid a twister, affable winker, toward the end no longer accepted
Skyrim missions, just explored and unlocked the map, maybe the best approximation of what was
my confounding life's trajectory, you loved the frenetic Carolina Chickadee, Ralph and Carter Stanley,
La Traviata, every opera, fish, shot coot from a keel, defended my blog against a vitriolic uncle, played
guitar, wore a hat, smoked for five years before quitting atop some waterfall (snap!) just like that.

National Museum of Mathematics

I text Woody, another poet, say meet me at the corner
of 26th and dull, Miles wants to learn about sums,
can you believe the son of two poets can't get enough
addition? I only found out my dad taught calculus for ten years
when I read his obituary. As a child I had zero concern
for the velocity of the goat or the boat or the river, but what
were they feeling, how did they differentiate? I was a terrible
tutee, hunched over our colonial kitchen table, solving for x and y,
pressing down hard into wood every wrong answer so that even
now I could trace the imprints of my errors had I chosen to
transport furniture across state lines. Miles is awed by mind
over measure, Woody hits a button to make a strobing sculpture
bloom. I become a human tree. I raise my arms, project smaller
copies of myself onto a wall, never-ending fractal.

III

January

I am too much in my body.
Mornings spent wishing for optical science and invisibility cloaks.
I dream of being pregnant again, even as I sweat through next-stage
luster.
The iced-over lake makes me miss something. Maybe the transparency
of water, the surprise of it having shadow.
My 84-year-old mother agrees to let me take her picture in front of the sign for
84 Lumber.
I need a heavy project to withstand a squall line.
The dog sits patiently in the snow. He wags his tail in it.
Patterns in the ice like enthusiastic errors.
I can't understand why *iamb* doesn't sound like the metrical foot it represents.
I am, I say, and my breath condenses.

Periodic

His final breaths
served as a reminder
that dying had been kept
from me all these years: Yes,
I wept, but more
because of the ecstatic
unbraiding that accompanied
the irregular pattern
of rapid gasps and
apnea—to witness
this interstice as flesh
shut down was sad
but extraordinary, to exist
between halt and
resumption meant
I could never go back to being
the daughter who only hours earlier
had found the vibrant green
underneath the oxidized
pesto unremarkable.

Easy

I qualify every search with easy.
Easy bean stew. Easy angel food cake.
What is easy to fix. What is healthy.

Easy training techniques for a needy
dog. Easy way to cross grief like a lake.
I qualify every search with easy.

Easy to understand recent study
on the brief fluke prints left in a whale's wake.
What is easy to fix. What is healthy.

Easy day trips from here. Easy journey
to see varying degrees of light break.
I qualify every search with easy.

Easy slumber. Easy to tell funny
jokes. Easiest way to conceal an ache.
What is easy to fix. What is healthy.

Easy upward trajectory. Dressy
pretend ease followed by the sharp intake.
I qualify every search with easy.
What is easy to fix. What is healthy.

Scotch Egg, Black Kazoo, Grandmother's Ghost

In the dream she wavers at the balustrade
mute bread-crumbed shaker in one hand
singing-drum in the other
makes me question what if I could never
again see myself
in a mirror
or a body of water
each stair charitable to her stepping
haze of agitation gathered just above
the cinched waist of her peplum dress
descending with awareness of a night
tornado being more difficult to confirm
part tree part me nettlesome
one third of a life spent
consolidating memory
here she seems to beg
take this kazoo
take this egg

Sea Glass

Mourn the empty space
the wrong talk fills.
Whale-ache made meet-cute.
Beachcombers roll in for the season.
Elsewhere, the season turns
colder. In light of safety
lamps the fur tops ride out
above the plantings—this is—what now—
a cursed ship or a shipped curse?

Addling

My father carried corn oil into dusk:
the translucent plastic like a lantern
held aloft, the yard pared down
immaculate—and overrun somehow
with a wild stamina. The light
was just ending. The geese were out,
feeding on the seeded grass. They lunged
the narrow slick of their bills
into the loam, weeded stalks
unmindful of the space between them,
the whites of their chin straps
impellent, unrehearsed, in rhythm to collective
hunger and inner-directed. Larger
than each bird alone I watched my father:
his stooped shadow, his flannel untucked
like a lake spilling over its banks. He moved
outside their periphery until he was nothing more
than pine, a mere familiar. Then I watched him
unscrew the cap and pour oil onto cloth,
lower into a nest of moss and feathers,
into a clutch of eggs I couldn't see
but knew was there.
The geese continued to eat.
The eggs absorbed the oil.
I tried to pick out the mother
while my father asphyxiated embryos,
his head turned towards the gaggle in humane
say-so. I wanted to feel her bristle.

He said she'd be misled into believing
the eggs would develop. That not knowing,
she would tend to them the same.

Perimenopause

I don't want to have another child, yet neither do I want the possibility of having another taken from me. In Persian mythology, a Peri is a winged spirit known for her beauty, at times mischievous, at times benevolent. If I listen to my body, I can hear hundreds of moody wings beating inside of me on iterations of the shoulders of the women I have been and even the babies I have lost. My first period started in a planetarium. The distance from the Earth to the sun is an *astronomical unit*, and I sometimes think of the growing space between each phase this way. The period before my father died happened unexpectedly in the hospital. His night nurse handed me a maternity pad. I put it on and thought about those initial days after giving birth, how a clot the size of a grapefruit was cause for concern but a tomato wasn't. I had already stained the chair I was curled up on, so I got a wet paper towel and wiped it down in view of the stars visible from the window my father was no longer aware of. His delirium meant we weren't alone, that spirits surrounded us. We talked to them together, and as I bled, I told him what I remembered of the planet Mercury, named after the winged God, how it moves quickly around the sun but spins slowly on its axis. Life is like that, the days long and the years short, or the days short and the years long, depending on the exact moment you ask someone.

My Parents' Lives Before Mine

I love anything so far off it feels near to me
        breeze half-stepping through the pines
as a girl I unearthed my mother's cruise ship album
        her narrow body pressed against a stranger's
in the Bahamas panorama like an ancient cup
        made more interesting
for being found in fragments I inherited
        my father's annotated textbooks I used
to annoy him with questions taking a fist
        through his raised *News & Observer* wondering
could the sails outside the frame withstand
        almost any wind condition there is
comfort in raking
        my fingers across the surface of deep
water devoid of sunlight why then am I
        hell-bent again on entering

There Are No Words

I know I cannot offer
language to approximate
your grief. Maybe
we could sit in silence
like translucent snailfish
that survive beneath the surface
of the ocean in extreme
depths. Or I could repeat
palindromes like *deified* and *solos*
as a kind of Möbius strip
of being. There is no comfort yet
but there is
Simona Kossack
who spent thirty years
in the Bialowieza Forest.
I could explain how she came up
with a device to alert wild animals
of a passing train. Maybe language
doesn't matter in moments
of life or death. Maybe sound alone
is enough to save us.

Moth Spotted Sipping a Sleeping Bird's Tears

Barbed straw lifted and plumbed the double lid,
pilfering salt from secluded corners.

Talc wings rustled in night reconnaissance.
Air attuned to what the mouth tasted, slip-

stream of sipping. Feeder, sleeper, watcher:
their configuration stirs a reader

in her distant kitchen. Insomniac
at the counter, she searches for the last

jalapeño, remembering the dream
of lightness, of becoming a maiden-

hair fern whose variegated fronds repel
wet. Wide awake in shadow, she finds it:

takes a knife and removes the fibrous stem,
curved proboscis, unsure if she's more moth,

bird, or scientific observer. Flight
feels like a foreign and improbable

essential. Even the quieted dream
of shed droplets attaches itself to

subterranean rhizome. She intends
to slice the pepper as a topper for

peanut butter toast. How her family
balks at that! More remarkable to touch

stem to the moistened inner triangle
of her right eye while seeing for the first

time her reflection in the blade's luster:
powder, feather, woman.

Parked Car

I don't have much time to write this poem, Yankee game on the radio, you on the soccer field in the purple evening light, it turns the jowls of a plott hound into a Renaissance fresco, windows lowered, a freshness permeates the air, hard to think that glacial worms exist, that your new best friend's father is a recent widower, I touch with gratitude the bruises on my wrist from where our puppy mouthed me, I brought him to my last therapy session, another screwup to talk about next week, lucky I am still here, why am I still here, why do some pennies get pressed into commemoration, the pitch is high, I have hardly any time to write, about thanks and arbitrariness, what gets tossed and what elongated, to tell the elusive world I love it, to put away my phone as you fling open the door, in the sudden dusk your knee bloody

Latter-Day Comfort

The sun sits tall without clothes on a riverbank
Gum chewing makes helium fall from a cloud
A flung coin is when you see colorful scents
Most loot actually buried its pirates
A space suit is born about every two seconds
Your heart is so hockey puck, so Rubik's Cube
The bones of many icebergs are a circus act
Still-life attacks take quick-handed depth
The air around horns weighs a whopping nest
There, there little one-quarter billboard
Here is the length of my warm fingerprint

Rare Bird

My niece is as old as my grief. She crawls toward an electrical outlet in one video and open arms in another. I keep trying to live my life with brightness, despite knowing the straw goat goes up in flames every Yule. Many dead wind up in a potter's field if they are buried at all. Nothing offsets my rage over the sale of a gun or the soda can tossed into a bird's nest. Then I remember: a Connecticut Warbler let me touch its plumage after my dad's funeral.

Uncountable

Garlic is an uncountable noun.
It can not be tallied as one garlic, two garlics, three. Tea
is another plural tease, like knowledge or evidence.
Politicians indifferent to contaminated water and polluted
air spend money, also uncountable. The more rearranged
furniture, the same singular. Vote with the courage of
innumerable anger, grown like garlic.

Love Island

When a man disrespects a woman he can leave
seashells on her vanity to apologize, say, *I tried
to collect the best ones*, write in bright red
lipstick on her mirror, *I miss our kisses*,
when a man denies the evidence
of it saying, *Are you kidding me*,
yes, he is falling in love with her, *her*
meaning indiscriminate attention, the sea
is amatory, it laps up the very shore
it erodes, it tumbles the shells a man
so easily gathered in acknowledgment of
a woman feeling bothered by him, delicate
broken spiral staircases all lined up in
an unadulterated row, doubled in the vanity
mirror, what is there to forgive even?

Lexaprode

Praise be to the little white pill
for confirming my interest in
going outside again this time
last year I was like a gravity
monger peddling low to only
myself my brain like the back
of a warped bookshelf the sign
on the way to recycling always
advertising *Surf & Turf & Hurt*
in my head a crocus was never
magical a woman on our street
rescued a ferret I couldn't even
focus on her story of how it
turned out to be a mink generic
escitalopram you surprised me
like the neon orange gel polish
I got this week that glows
in the dark I thought we were
having a lightning storm it was
my hands tucking in my son *danke*
daily 5mg construction worker
sweating in the heat to wave me
through expediently the truth is
my father died we never know
what's coming next when God closes
a window He opens a door
He sometimes rips the roof right
off a doublewide

Thank You

Thank you for dying in summer
Sprinkler dotting my sleeveless dress
Strawberries staining my fingers
It's an illusion that we get to choose but still
Thank you for first slipping away
During the season of
Sumo oranges
Eastern redbud
Could I have tightened your belt
Around your disappearing frame while
Snow pelted the window
Not sure I could have summoned
The courage to ask you
Are you scared to die
Would you rather
Have written your name
In the sky
Or on a grain of rice
How did those early pioneers do it
Fire borrowed in cast-iron pans
Rope strung between whited out house and barn
When you suddenly sat up in bed
And asked me
Shall we gather at the river
Arms dancing
That final night when I placed
Ice wrapped in washcloths

On your face and groin
Spine visible like guides on a fishing pole
Thank you for
The warm air outside for how it
Smelled like sweet gardenias

Idiot Birdwalk

Our guide offers to let us take a peek through his high-powered
telescope at a common loon, and my son asks, *Why would we,
if it's common?* I love his humor but not at 9 a.m. when I'm here
to see a blue-winged teal. I've lent him my dad's binoculars,

which hang around his neck like an albatross. *Can we go now?*
he demands, just as an elderly enthusiast explains how a bluebird
nest is organized like a designer cup. When my son was four,
he climbed into a $500 checkered urn at the MacKenzie-

Childs showroom. I am mostly either trying to convince him
to get out or stay put. Our guide points to a subdued female
red-wing blackbird who looks as though she fixed the wrong color
mac and cheese for someone. I didn't think my son thought about

my dad at all, until he molded him out of clay for a My Life diorama.
Please just do this for me, I plead, and he runs away, yells, *Idiot
birdwalk!* The common loon was dwarfed by a boat, but still,
I wanted him to show interest in a distant black speck. I miss the people

I've lost. Where did they go? It hurts to raise my eyes to the blinding sky
to try and spot a double-crested cormorant, so instead I turn
my binoculars on my son, now peering through his own at the water.

Resurrection

It's my mother's birthday and Easter Sunday.
At the Chinese buffet, she piles her plate high with shrimp
and oysters while I take a lap to rule out any
room-temperature chicken. My son gives her a notebook
he purchased at Staples because nothing else
was open. At the table, there is light talk
of the resurrection. When Jesus approached
Mary Magdalene outside the tomb, she mistook him
for the gardener. My mother enjoys this detail. My father
died eight month ago; shortly after, she collapsed
and survived two weeks on a ventilator. Her heart
stopped but they got it going again. A brightly-colored
spare rib speared on her fork, she reflects on a recent
wave of thefts at her senior living facility. *Ethel sleeps
with a chair propped up against her door, but it's all
kind of exciting.* My son suggests, *Use the notebook
to jot down clues.* The confines of her world
have shifted. *I'd love another ice cream*, she says,
then tells us how she asked the greenhouse manager
for a spider plant and fern to take care of.

Anniversary

It's been a week
and I still can't scrub my age
from my right calf where
the triathlon official
scrawled it. I've been marking
time since you left us
by doing things. Some
might make you
proud, although what
does a slipstream care
about splits? The pooling
blood in the dependent
parts of your body marked
them red and purple. Before
that, you picked at bed sheets
like you were a buoy-
liberator. Last month,
in Yeats' tower, a docent told me
she suspects Georgie
fabricated her occult connections
just to keep her husband
near her. Which is sadder:
a pretend seance where you know
the truth or talking to the air
without a clue?

Homestay

I circle back to nature camp with your forgotten water shoes. A decade ago, I journeyed by canvas truck from Tena to Pimpilala. Our driver recommended we elevate our rain boots to prevent scorpions from crawling inside them. A Quichua family welcomed us into their wooden huts. For five days, I didn't tell a soul why I'd come, other than I was a travel agent. I drank pilsners as big as my forearm, afterwards checked the toilet seat for fire ants. Suspended in the nebulous space between self and stranger, in the Amazon, I shared a cigarette with a retired Russian bus operator who claimed Malarone made him hallucinate his route. Our group played Yahtzee by candlelight; we swore it was a game of luck. The teenage daughter of our host family nursed her newborn in a corner. A shaman fashioned a thick poultice, said he derived both sunrise and sunset from the cedar. Using his fingers, he painted our cheeks with red from the achiote pod, a different symbol for each visitor: Mine was Mother Earth. On a dance floor in Quito, the night before our departure, I yelled over EDM to finally tell the two young Brits that I'd had three miscarriages in six months. The women stopped moving. They held me to a looping beat. Before jumping up and down again, the one highest on coke touched my cheek, the spot where the achiote still was, and said, *You're going to make an incredible mum.*

Men

The one who delivered me and the one who raised me.
The one who once compared me unfavorably to his beauty
queen ex. The one who spoke as a bellwether, who mistook my ambition
for sadness. The boatel one night one. The one entirely cylinders
and go, the anti-hero. The one who said *wings* and my wings would spread.
Memoranda one followed by aloof one. The one who asked if he could
put it in and the one who didn't bother asking. The one who covered me
like mint. Friend's couch one, proscenium one, blunts one. Black out
one. Black out one again. All the good ones I wanted to save and the bad
tipper ones. The one who spit on me in Brooklyn and the one with a gun
who robbed me in Barcelona. The one with a pocketknife I kicked
in the face in that same city two years later. The one I thought was
the one, then the one I married, the one who holds my hand through
every complication. The son who will one day become one.

You Ask Me to Tell You the Story

Your birth was like hearing
a distant player piano
and catching my breath while under
cathedral glass in retrospect
the full moon was
crescent my labor
nurse wore a silver bean
necklace identical to
mine I held you
like a squirming catamaran
like a solid radio I got right
down to field work you took
forever to appear in an inch
of time you materialized I cried
from the sheer natural
terror of it fully-loaded
sub tasted good after
mixed with aromatic blood I
loved you instantaneously I
turned away from your eyes
preferring the memory
of skin on abdomen first
latch easier than imagining
the years ahead hard
to conceive of the night
nine summers later
you would climb into my lap
confused by the silent

film on the inflatable screen
outside you can never get enough
of words you whispered in my ear
tell me the story

Closing

We stayed until the very last minute
of the very last day of the season, until
the lifeguard blew his whistle as a final
salvo, and the yellowjackets gathered
in prayer around an electric blue freeze
pop, and the air above the pool turned
harmonic like someone had barely
pressed their finger to the late afternoon—
        Years ago, on a ferry to Aegina,
        I struck up a conversation with an Athenian
        who was a landscape artist, and when I asked him,
        Are you planning on painting there?
        he answered, *Not enough time. I'd rather live*
        the water. I think about that moment
whenever I am on the verge of anything hindmost,
or ending, or closing, like dipping a toe in
in anticipatory recollection.

First Day

My son was nine days late. It took
the threat of induction to convince him
to leave my carriage. Now, with limbs
like umbels, he bears his own
bloom. Fingertips stained dark
from blueberries, he decamps
at a clip, weaves between September
bees on his way to a place that isn't
pear-shaped. Last summer, we posed
with our heads emerging from behind
stolen marble torsos. The body that was
my body, suddenly this other.

Warble

The way to play the theremin is to never touch
the instrument. Interference creates melody. Even
swaying can alter the electromagnetic field.
Our house shakes from the vibration of trucks
on the deteriorating highway. I mostly feel
these tremors in the bedroom when I set out
to write, distracted by the sound of a circular
saw or the shadows made by moving hands
in videos of theremin players. I prefer not knowing
what will come next. Like how a curved mirror
gathers and concentrates light, the distance
between what I intend to write and what
I actually do is a kind of confirmation
and faith in prospect, in span, in air.

Loss

I prefer the desiccated pod to the moony flower. You can make a starfish out of five halves glued together at the base or a holiday garland strung with sweetgum balls that save. What's more compelling than an empty shell? The winter after my dad died, he tapered to a point, I power-walked past a house whose overhanging second-story Christmas lights were arranged like strings on a missing harp. The most alive I feel is when I corner dearth. To hold in my hands what isn't, like the time our son brought home a drawing labeled, *Self-Portrait of What I'm Not*. My dad coughed up phlegm into a hospital napkin stained with grease. I'd smuggled bacon to give him a final taste of fat. He couldn't swallow, just held it in his mouth, smiling. I knew in that moment of floating goose down, third time in a month our rescue dog turned and tore into my body, that we had to give her up. To love anything wholly is to accept its painful winding loss. But you can make a cradle out of a milkweed pod, use the floss as swaddling for an acorn baby.

Hawks on Light Posts

Downstairs, my husband practices
"Jingle Bells" in a minor key.
I feel a dollop of despondency

but soon lose it. I search for a map
of the highest point in each state
for Secret Santa. *Do you find yourself missing*

exits because you are staring at the mountains?
I do seem to be looking up more often.
In November, I gleefully hunted my family

with foam-tipped arrows at a lodge
in Pennsylvania. Miraculously, we won
three times at bingo. I shared a bed with my mom.

Sometimes, our feet touched. I fell asleep thinking
about a disappearing glass. She woke me
to ask, *How did that illusionist make the table float?*

Even in the dark, our grief got away from us,
barely on a tether. I can no longer tell
if it's high up or low down when I laugh.

For months after the Battle of Gettysburg,
residents rubbed peppermint oil under their noses
to mask the stench of rotting bodies.

My father is as far away as a relic
hidden in a field prohibited from detectorists.
The air I take in is crisp, clear.

I only prevailed upon his spirit for the winning
letter and number. A losing woman
to my right leaned in and confided,

I lost my heart a year ago.
He came back to me as hawks on light posts.
My grief has flown off and alighted somewhere

I cannot see, although I call out for it.

Triptych

I

Outside of Franco's, I extend my free palm to a pomeranian gray around the eyes. His owner tells me he is still a puppy, that after his mother got run over, his fur turned ashen. *He stopped eating. He waited by the door.* I'm holding a can of sparkling water with the disclaimer *naturally flavored with other natural flavors*, which prompts me to offer, *It's too much.*

II

When our son was 15 months, he failed a light refraction test. The doctor referred us to an ophthalmologist for an emergency appointment: *It could be an error, but it could also be retinoblastoma.* For 24 hours, I thought about nothing but *red reflex*, the term I had just learned for what it means to have healthy pupil reflection. I combed through old photos of him looking for any absence. I shut out the sun and shone a flashlight in his face until he wailed.

III

My dad closed his eyes the day before he died and never opened them again. I had thought I would be the one to lower his lids. I had practiced on my own in the Best Western Plus, pulling down the skin until it made a satisfying *click* like a tin of anchovies opened incrementally. Now that you have fully entered and left the poem, I see you trying it yourself.

PUBLICATION ACKNOWLEDGMENTS

I am grateful to the editors of the following publications in which the following poems in this book first appeared:

8 Poems ("Homeschool")

805 Lit + Art ("First Day")

Best New Poets 2015 ("The Last Travel Agent")

Best New Poets 2023 ("G Day")

Small Harbor Publishing anthology *Braving the Body* ("Giving Birth May Alter a Mother's Bones")

Cider House Press ("Rare Bird")

december ("The Vine")

DMQ Review ("Perimenopause")

Euphony ("Periodic")

Fairy Tale Review ("Legs")

FIELD ("Hot Horse")

The Garlic Press ("Lexaprode")

Gulf Coast ("Addling")

jubilat ("Sea Glass")

Leveler ("Open Water")

The Lunar Journal ("Migration")

One Art ("Easy" and "The Surprise")

Quarter After Eight ("Commerce in Absence")

Raleigh Review ("Parked Car")

River Styx ("January," "The Thirteenth Guest," "Pod," and "Alternate")

Sixth Finch ("America Runs On")

Subnivean ("Moth Spotted Sipping a Sleeping Bird's Tears" and "Warble")

SWWIM ("Cans &")

Tupleo Press anthology *The Last Milkweed* ("Loss")

PERSONAL ACKNOWLEDGMENTS

"Hot Horse" is for poet Tomaž Šalamun, who made Ljubljana a magical city. "Idiot Birdwalk" is for poet Colie Hoffman, who I still look for every day. "Moth Spotted Sipping a Sleeping Bird's Tears" is for Shilo McGiff and her incandescent mind. Thank you Sharon Olds and Kimiko Hahn for the immeasurable wisdom you imparted that I could only begin to implement decades later. Woody Loverude, I am grateful for your years of friendship and your willingness to accompany my child to the National Museum of Mathematics. Thank you Linzi Garcia and Tracy Million Simmons for ushering *Warble* into the world, and Caryn Mirriam-Goldberg for picking it. I owe my beautiful cover design to Richard Kegler and to my dad's high school arithmetic homework, which he mysteriously left to me in a bank safe deposit box. I owe my author photo to Macy Smolsky, whose discerning eye is only matched by her empathy. Meg Peck: Thank you for being a stand-up therapist. Dan and Miles: I love you more than poems can say. Mom and Dad: None of this would be possible without you.

ABOUT THE AUTHOR

Alicia Rebecca Myers is a poet and essayist who holds an MFA in Poetry from NYU, where she was a Goldwater Writing Fellow. Her writing has appeared in publications that include *Best New Poets*, *Creative Nonfiction*, *FIELD*, *River Styx*, *Gulf Coast*, *SWWIM*, *december*, *Rattle*, and *The Rumpus*. Her chapbook of poems, *My Seaborgium* (Brain Mill Press, 2016), was selected as a winner of the inaugural Mineral Point Chapbook Series, and she has been the recipient of a Kimmel Harding Nelson residency for poetry and a Looking Glass Rock Writers' Conference nonfiction scholarship. *Warble* is her first full-length book.

Meadowlark POETRY

Books are a way to explore, connect, and discover. Poetry incites us to observe and think in new ways, bridging our understanding of the world with our artistic need to interact with, shape, and share it with others.

Publishing poetry is our way of saying:
We love these words,
we want to preserve them,
we want to play a role in sharing them
with the world.

Meadowlark Press
— since 2014 —

meadowlarkpoetrypress.com

Follow Meadowlark Press
on Facebook & Instagram

f facebook.com/ReadAMeadowlarkBook

⊙ @meadowlarkbooks

BIRDY POETRY PRIZE WINNERS

2023
Turkey Vulture
Zachary Lundgren

"At first, the poems [. . .] seem like a portal to another place and time—a small town, a lifetime ago. [. . .] Zachary Lundgren reminds us that there's no veil between the past and the present. [. . .] In one sense we aren't who we were in our youth. In another, we absolutely are. We are every version of ourselves we've ever been and ever will be."
–Melissa Fite Johnson, 2023 Birdy Poetry Prize Judge, author of *Green*

2022
Cupping Our Palms
Jonathan Greenhause

"These provocative, trustworthy poems owe their strength to narrators who are not afraid to confront their own sense of awe, misgivings, and incredulity, as it pertains to their various stations in life. The prevailing subject of parenthood, and what it means to shepherd children through the stages of growth, keeps circling in this superb collection."
–Bart Edelman, 2022 Birdy Poetry Prize Judge, author of *Whistling to Trick the Wind*

2021
Knowing Is a Branching Trail
Alison Hicks

"*Knowing Is a Branching Trail* captured my attention. I read in search of moments that create a soft pause in me. Time given back to me that allows me to sit with feeling, safely and freely. There were voices in the work that transitioned from stranger to companion. It felt as if we shared an understanding. [. . .] I felt less alone with this book."
–Huascar Medina, 2021 Birdy Poetry Prize Judge, Poet Laureate of Kansas (2019-2022), author of *Un Mango Grows in Kansas*

2020
Selected Poems: 2000-2020
JC Mehta

"This Selected group of poems illuminates some harsh realities regarding identity. There are poems that smack a consciousness sideways. The poems have a real grit to them. For the reader, each poem will be an eye-opening experience."
–Stanley E. Banks, 2020 Birdy Poetry Prize Judge, author of *Blue Beat Syncopation*

2019
A Certain Kind of Forgiveness
Carol Kapaun Ratchenski

"There is a worldliness in these poems, the kind of grit that accompanies a strong heart. There's awareness–of the self, of the world. And the poems are populated with the magical, husky things of this earth: warm beer in Berlin, rice in a bowl in a monastery, and stains from fresh cranberries. These are poems we can savor, now and again."
–Kevin Rabas, Poet Laureate of Kansas (2017-2019), author of *More Than Words*

Meadowlark Press created The Birdy Poetry Prize to celebrate the voices of our era. Cash prize, publication, and 50 copies awarded annually.

Accepting Entries: September 1 - December 1
Entry Fee: $25
Prize: $1,000 cash, publication by Meadowlark Press, 50 copies of the completed book

All entries will be considered for standard Meadowlark publishing contract offers, as well.

Full-length poetry manuscripts (55-page minimum) will be considered. Poems may be previously published in journals and/or anthologies, but not in full-length single-author volumes. Poets are eligible to enter, regardless of publishing history.

See www.meadowlarkbookstore.com for complete submission guidelines.